Take Cont
Your Life

How to Silence Fear and Win the
Mental Game

ISBN 978-1-300-40722-5
Mel Robbins
Copyright@2025

TABLE OF CONTENT

CHAPTER 1

Understanding Fear

The Nature of Fear

Fear is one of the most primal and instinctive emotions, deeply ingrained in human evolution and psychology. It acts as a double-edged sword—on one side, it protects us from potential harm; on the other, it can inhibit growth and hinder decision-making when misunderstood or left unchecked. To understand the complexities of fear, we must first explore its definition and evolutionary role, as well as its influence on the human experience.
Definition of Fear

Fear is an emotional and physiological response to a perceived threat. It triggers the body's "fight, flight, or freeze" response, preparing an individual to either confront the danger, escape from it, or momentarily immobilize themselves to avoid detection. It's important to note that fear stems from perception—meaning that the threat doesn't have to be real; it only needs to feel real to elicit fear.

From a psychological perspective, fear encompasses both conscious and subconscious elements. For instance, you may feel a racing heart and clammy hands when standing near the edge of a high cliff (a conscious awareness of danger).

Alternatively, fear can emerge from less tangible sources, such as apprehension about an uncertain future or doubt in your abilities—these tend to operate at a deeper, subconscious level.

The Evolutionary Role of Fear

Fear has played an essential role in the survival of the human species. In prehistoric times, humans faced myriad life-threatening dangers, such as predators, harsh weather, and scarce resources. Fear acted as an internal alarm system, sharpening the senses and enabling quick decision-making in the face of immediate threats. For example:

Physical Protection: Fear signaled ancient humans to flee from lions, snakes, or other predators.

Social Cohesion: Fear of exile or ostracism from a tribe reinforced behaviors that promoted group survival.

This survival mechanism is hardwired into the amygdala, a small almond-shaped structure in the brain that processes emotional reactions. When the amygdala perceives a threat, it signals the release of stress hormones like adrenaline and cortisol, which heighten physical preparedness. While this response was crucial in prehistoric times, modern humans rarely encounter the same immediate life-or-death situations. Yet, the fear mechanism remains intact and often overreacts to non-lethal threats, such as public speaking, failing an exam, or disappointing others.

The Dual Nature of Fear: Helpful vs. Hindering

The role of fear in modern human life can be categorized into two contrasting functions: protection and inhibition.

Fear as a Protector

Enhancing Awareness: Fear forces us to assess our surroundings and anticipate risks. For example, feeling uneasy when walking alone at night encourages vigilance.

Encouraging Preparation: Anticipatory fear, such as anxiety before a major exam or presentation, motivates us to prepare thoroughly.

Facilitating Survival Instincts: Even in contemporary times, fear can save lives— think of how quickly we react to avoid a car accident when fear kicks in.

Fear as a Hindrance

Paralysis and Overthinking: Fear of making the wrong decision can lead to analysis paralysis, where no action is taken due to overwhelming uncertainty.

Limiting Potential: Fear of failure or rejection often prevents people from pursuing their dreams, such as starting a new business or sharing creative ideas.

Impacting Mental Health: Chronic fear or anxiety can lead to issues like depression, insomnia, and substance abuse.

Recognizing when fear is helpful versus when it becomes harmful is a key step toward taking control of your life.
Fear in a Modern Context

The triggers for fear have evolved alongside human society. Today, fear is often more psychological than physical, fueled by the complexity and pace of modern life.
Common modern fears include:

Fear of Change: Humans find comfort in routines and familiarity, making change—whether in career, relationships, or identity—a significant source of fear.

Fear of Rejection: Social validation remains deeply important, and rejection can feel like a threat to one's sense of belonging.

Fear of Failure: With societal emphasis on achievement, the fear of failing to meet expectations looms large.

Fear of the Unknown: The unpredictability of life events, such as economic downturns, pandemics, or personal crises, generates widespread anxiety.

Interestingly, while these fears are less about immediate survival, they can evoke the same intensity of response as if one were in physical danger.

Fear's Influence on Decision-Making

The ways in which fear impacts decisions can vary widely. In some situations, fear sharpens focus and ensures caution. However, it can also cloud judgment and create irrational behaviors. Examples include:

Overestimating Threats: Fear can magnify the perceived severity of a situation, causing overreaction. For instance, fear of flying may overshadow the statistically low likelihood of an airplane crash.

Avoidance Behavior: Fear often leads individuals to avoid challenges altogether, missing opportunities for growth.

Confirmation Bias: Fear of certain outcomes may cause people to seek information that reinforces their fears, rather than challenging their assumptions.

The Social and Cultural Role of Fear

Fear is not only an individual experience but also a collective one. Social and cultural norms shape what people fear and how they respond to it. For instance:

In individualistic societies, there may be greater fear of personal failure or not living up to one's potential.

In collectivist cultures, fear may center more around dishonoring family or community values.

Media and technology also amplify fears, with sensational headlines and viral misinformation creating an environment of constant anxiety.

Understanding these influences can help individuals critically assess whether their fears are self-generated or shaped by external factors.
Transforming the Role of Fear

To take control of your life, the role of fear must shift from being a dominant force to a constructive one. Strategies for achieving this include:

Acknowledgment: Accepting fear as a natural and universal emotion rather than denying it.

Contextualization: Assessing whether the perceived threat is realistic and proportional to the reaction.

Empowerment: Viewing fear as an opportunity to build resilience and courage, rather than as an obstacle.

Types of Fear

Fear is not a one-size-fits-all emotion. While its roots lie in survival, its manifestations in modern life can be complex and deeply personal. Let's delve into three of the most common types of fear—fear of change, fear of rejection, and fear of being alone—and examine their origins, effects, and strategies to overcome them.

Fear of Change

Definition and Roots: The fear of change stems from our innate preference for stability and predictability. Change, by definition, disrupts the familiar. Whether it's a new job, moving to a different city, or even shifting personal beliefs, change requires stepping into the unknown. This can trigger a cascade of doubts and anxieties, as the brain interprets unfamiliarity as a potential threat.

From an evolutionary perspective, humans thrived by relying on established routines and patterns. These provided a sense of safety and efficiency in resource allocation. While modern life may not require us to hunt or gather, the brain still clings to predictability as a form of comfort.

Manifestations: Fear of change often presents as procrastination, resistance to new opportunities, or an overwhelming desire to stick to what's always worked. People may:

Avoid taking risks, even when the potential reward is great.

Sabotage progress by clinging to old habits or relationships.

Experience heightened anxiety or stress when faced with uncertainty.

Effects: While staying in one's comfort zone can feel safe, it also stifles growth and innovation. Fear of change can lead to missed opportunities, stagnation, and dissatisfaction over time. It can prevent individuals from discovering their true potential or pursuing their dreams.

Strategies to Overcome Fear of Change:

Reframe Change as Growth: Instead of focusing on what could go wrong, imagine the possibilities that change might bring. Ask yourself: "What's the best-case scenario?"

Take Incremental Steps: Break down the change into smaller, manageable actions. This reduces the overwhelming nature of big transitions.

Build a Support System: Surround yourself with people who encourage and support your journey, providing reassurance during times of doubt.

Embrace Curiosity: View change as an opportunity to learn and explore, rather than a challenge to endure.

Fear of Rejection

Definition and Roots: At its core, the fear of rejection is the fear of being excluded or deemed unworthy. This fear has deep evolutionary roots, as early humans depended on belonging to social groups for survival. Being ostracized from the group often meant facing dangers alone, reducing the chances of survival. While modern life doesn't present the same physical risks, the psychological need for acceptance remains.

The fear of rejection often ties into self-worth. It can arise from past experiences of being excluded, criticized, or ignored, leading to heightened sensitivity to situations that might result in similar outcomes.

Manifestations: Fear of rejection can manifest in various ways, including:

Avoiding social interactions or public speaking due to the possibility of criticism.

Overcompensating by seeking constant approval or validation from others.

Hesitating to pursue romantic relationships, friendships, or career opportunities.

People-pleasing behaviors, where one sacrifices their own needs to gain acceptance.

Effects: Living in fear of rejection can erode confidence and authenticity. It can lead to:

Suppressing one's true opinions, desires, or talents to conform to perceived expectations.

Isolation, as one avoids situations that could lead to rejection.

A cycle of self-doubt and negative self-talk, further lowering self-esteem.

Strategies to Overcome Fear of Rejection:
Challenge Negative Beliefs: Remind yourself
that rejection is not a reflection of your
worth but often a matter of circumstance or
preference.

Normalize Rejection: Understand that
everyone faces rejection—it's a natural part
of life. Even the most successful individuals
have encountered setbacks.

Practice Vulnerability: Start small by sharing
your thoughts or feelings with trusted
individuals. Gradually, you'll build resilience
to rejection.

Focus on Self-Worth: Cultivate self-
acceptance and self-love, so that your sense
of worth isn't tied to external validation.

Fear of Being Alone

Definition and Roots: The fear of being alone
is rooted in humans' deeply social nature.
Historically, isolation from the tribe was a
significant risk to survival. Today, while
physical survival doesn't depend on constant
social interaction, emotional well-being often
does. Loneliness is associated with feelings
of emptiness, worthlessness, and
disconnection.

This fear can arise from various experiences,
such as childhood neglect, the loss of close
relationships, or societal pressures to
maintain an active social life. It can also

stem from internal struggles, such as not feeling comfortable or at peace with oneself. Manifestations: Fear of being alone may lead to:

Staying in unhealthy or toxic relationships to avoid loneliness.
Distracting oneself constantly with social media, entertainment, or activities to avoid quiet moments.

Experiencing anxiety at the thought of solitude, even for short periods.

Difficulty making independent decisions, as validation from others feels essential.

Effects: While connection is vital for mental and emotional health, an excessive fear of being alone can hinder personal growth and self-discovery. It can lead to:

Codependency in relationships, where one relies heavily on others for emotional support.

Burnout from overextending oneself socially to avoid solitude.

Inability to develop a strong sense of self, as time alone provides space for introspection and clarity.

Strategies to Overcome Fear of Being Alone:

Redefine Solitude: View alone time as an opportunity for self-care and reflection rather than a punishment.
Build a Healthy Relationship with Yourself: Spend time exploring your interests, passions, and goals without external influence.

Gradually Face Solitude: Start by dedicating short periods of time to being alone, engaging in activities that bring you joy or peace.

Strengthen Your Support Network: While solitude is important, maintaining meaningful relationships ensures you don't feel isolated.

The Impact of Fear

Fear is a deeply ingrained emotion that influences nearly every aspect of our lives. While it serves a vital evolutionary purpose, its impact can extend far beyond immediate survival. Fear often takes an emotional, mental, and physical toll, and it can distort decision-making and hold people back from reaching their full potential. Understanding these impacts is crucial for learning to manage fear effectively and reclaiming control over life.
Emotional, Mental, and Physical Tolls of Fear

Emotional Toll Fear's emotional effects can be both immediate and long-lasting. It creates a sense of unease, anxiety, or dread that can undermine a person's ability to feel secure and at peace. The emotional toll of fear manifests in several ways:

Anxiety and Worry: Fear often triggers constant worry about worst-case scenarios, even in situations with little actual risk. This overthinking can lead to chronic anxiety.

Low Self-Esteem: Persistent fear—whether it's fear of failure, rejection, or judgment—can erode self-confidence and create feelings of inadequacy.

Emotional Instability: Living in fear fosters a rollercoaster of emotions, from bouts of helplessness to frustration and anger. It often leaves individuals feeling emotionally drained.

Avoidance and Detachment: Fear prompts people to withdraw from challenging situations or avoid relationships to sidestep the risk of hurt or failure. Over time, this leads to isolation and a reduced capacity for emotional connection.

These emotional burdens not only hinder personal happiness but also create a ripple effect, influencing relationships, productivity, and overall well-being.

Mental Toll The mental impact of fear is far-reaching, as it fundamentally alters cognitive processes. Fear distorts perception, biases judgment, and disrupts focus, leaving individuals trapped in a cycle of negativity. The mental toll includes:

Overthinking: Fear causes the mind to dwell excessively on risks, amplifying real or imagined problems.

Impaired Focus: Persistent fear monopolizes mental bandwidth, making it difficult to concentrate on tasks or enjoy life's pleasures.

Catastrophic Thinking: Fear can lead to exaggerating the consequences of potential failures, pushing individuals into a spiral of worst-case scenario thinking.

Insecurity and Indecision: Fear undermines the ability to make confident decisions, as it clouds judgment with doubt and hesitation.

Stress and Cognitive Fatigue: Chronic fear keeps the brain in a hyper-vigilant state, eventually leading to mental exhaustion and decreased problem-solving ability.

Left unchecked, the mental effects of fear can become overwhelming, reinforcing negative thought patterns and self-doubt.

Physical Toll Fear doesn't just exist in the mind—it manifests in the body as well. The connection between fear and the physical body is rooted in the brain's stress response system, particularly the amygdala and the hypothalamus. This connection produces several physiological effects:

Increased Stress Hormones: Fear triggers the release of adrenaline and cortisol, which prepare the body for fight or flight. Prolonged exposure to these hormones leads to chronic stress, which negatively impacts health.

Physical Symptoms: Sweating, a racing heart, trembling, shortness of breath, and muscle tension are common physical manifestations of acute fear.

Weakened Immune System: Chronic fear can suppress the immune system, making individuals more susceptible to illnesses.

Impact on Cardiovascular Health: Sustained stress caused by fear increases the risk of hypertension, heart disease, and other cardiovascular issues.

Fatigue and Sleep Disturbances: The body's constant state of alertness due to fear can lead to insomnia and fatigue, which further impair physical and mental health.

Overall, the physical toll of fear is a reminder of its far-reaching influence, underscoring the need to address and manage it effectively.
How Fear Distorts Decision-Making and Limits Potential

Fear doesn't just affect our emotions and bodies—it actively influences the decisions we make and the direction our lives take. It creates mental roadblocks that keep individuals stuck in their comfort zones, unable to embrace opportunities for growth and change.

Distortion of Decision-Making Fear distorts decision-making by shifting focus away from logic and possibility, and toward perceived risks and dangers. This distortion manifests in several ways:

Risk Aversion: Fear magnifies potential risks and downplays potential rewards, making individuals overly cautious or hesitant to take even calculated risks.

Example: A person may avoid applying for a dream job because they fear rejection, even if they're well-qualified.

Avoidance Behavior: Fear encourages people to sidestep uncomfortable decisions entirely, hoping the issue will resolve itself or disappear.

Example: A fear of confrontation might prevent someone from addressing critical issues in a personal or professional relationship.

Short-Term Thinking: Fear creates a sense of urgency that prioritizes immediate relief over long-term benefits.

Example: Staying in a dissatisfying job may feel safer in the short term but stifles personal growth and happiness in the long run.

Confirmation Bias: Fear can lead individuals to seek out information that reinforces their doubts and anxieties, further entrenching negative beliefs.

These distortions create a self-fulfilling cycle, where avoidance and indecision exacerbate the very situations people hope to escape.

Limitation of Potential Fear is one of the greatest barriers to personal growth and fulfillment. By amplifying doubts and insecurities, fear keeps individuals from stepping into their true potential. Some key ways fear limits potential include:

Missed Opportunities: Fear of failure, judgment, or rejection often prevents people from seizing opportunities that could lead to significant personal or professional growth.

Example: Fear might discourage someone from starting a new business, traveling to an unfamiliar place, or expressing their creativity.

Stagnation: Fear fosters a preference for the status quo, where comfort takes precedence over progress. As a result, people remain stuck in unfulfilling situations.

Example: Staying in a toxic relationship or career path because change seems too daunting.

Lack of Authenticity: Fear of judgment or rejection often leads individuals to suppress

their true selves, conforming to others'
expectations instead of embracing their
unique identities.

Example: Fear may cause someone to hide
their passions or beliefs, even at the cost of
personal satisfaction.

Erosion of Confidence: Fear chips away at
self-confidence, creating a cycle of self-doubt
that reinforces perceived limitations.

Ultimately, fear limits potential by convincing
individuals to settle for less than they're
capable of achieving. It tells them that the
risks of failure outweigh the rewards of
success, preventing them from pursuing
meaningful goals.
Breaking the Cycle of Fear

To mitigate the emotional, mental, and
physical tolls of fear and reduce its impact
on decision-making, it's essential to develop
tools and strategies that foster courage and
resilience:

Mindfulness and Awareness: By becoming
aware of fear's presence, individuals can
separate genuine threats from imagined
ones and address them more rationally.

Positive Action: Small, intentional steps
toward feared situations can help build
confidence and reduce avoidance behavior
over time.

Support Networks: Friends, mentors, or professionals can provide reassurance, guidance, and encouragement in the face of fear.

Reframing: Viewing fear as a sign of opportunity rather than danger fosters a growth mindset.

CHAPTER 2

Common Mental Battles

Imposter Syndrome

Imposter Syndrome is a pervasive psychological experience characterized by chronic self-doubt, feelings of inadequacy, and the belief that one's accomplishments are undeserved. Despite evidence of competence, individuals with imposter syndrome often attribute their success to external factors such as luck, timing, or others' overestimation of their abilities. This phenomenon affects people from all walks of life, including high achievers, students, professionals, and creatives. Here, we will explore how to recognize self-doubt and inadequacy as it relates to imposter syndrome and distinguish impostor thoughts from reality.
Recognizing Self-Doubt and Feelings of Inadequacy

1. The Roots of Imposter Syndrome: Imposter syndrome often stems from early experiences, environmental factors, or societal pressures. Common causes include:

High Expectations: Growing up in an environment that prioritized perfectionism or excellence may lead to internalized pressure to constantly prove oneself.

Comparison Culture: In a world driven by social media and relentless comparisons, individuals may feel inadequate when measuring their successes against curated portrayals of others' lives.

Stereotype Threats: People from marginalized groups, such as women in male-dominated fields or underrepresented minorities, may experience heightened imposter syndrome due to societal biases and stereotypes.

New Challenges: Major life transitions or career advancements—such as starting a new job or assuming a leadership position—can evoke fears of inadequacy.

Understanding the origins of imposter syndrome is essential in recognizing its presence and addressing its impact.

2. Manifestations of Self-Doubt: Self-doubt tied to imposter syndrome manifests in various ways, including:

Attributing Success to Luck: Individuals downplay their achievements, believing external circumstances, rather than their efforts, were responsible.

Fear of Being Exposed as a Fraud: There's a persistent fear that others will "find out" they are incompetent or undeserving of their position.

Overworking to Compensate: To prove themselves, individuals may overprepare, overperform, or sacrifice personal well-being. Difficulty Accepting Praise: Compliments or recognition are often met with discomfort, deflection, or disbelief.

Minimizing Accomplishments: People with imposter syndrome may undermine their own achievements or consider them insignificant compared to others.

Perfectionism: A constant pursuit of flawlessness can reinforce feelings of inadequacy when minor imperfections occur.

Recognizing these patterns is the first step toward addressing self-doubt and reclaiming confidence.

3. The Emotional Impact of Inadequacy: Living with imposter syndrome takes a toll on emotional well-being, often leading to:

Chronic Stress: The fear of being exposed as a fraud can create constant tension and anxiety.

Low Self-Esteem: Repeatedly doubting oneself reinforces feelings of unworthiness.

Burnout: Overworking to compensate for perceived inadequacies can lead to exhaustion and diminished productivity.

Missed Opportunities: Self-doubt may prevent individuals from pursuing challenges, promotions, or creative endeavors.

By identifying these emotional impacts, individuals can better understand the ways in which imposter syndrome may be holding them back.

Differentiating Impostor Thoughts from Reality

1. Understanding the Nature of Impostor Thoughts: Impostor thoughts are irrational beliefs rooted in fear and insecurity, rather than factual evidence. Examples of such thoughts include:

"I'm not as smart/talented/capable as everyone thinks I am."

"I only got this opportunity because I was lucky, not because I earned it."

"It's just a matter of time before people realize I don't belong here."

These thoughts often exist in direct conflict with reality, where tangible evidence supports an individual's competence and achievements.

2. Challenging Cognitive Distortions: To differentiate impostor thoughts from reality, it's important to recognize and challenge cognitive distortions—irrational ways of thinking that reinforce self-doubt. Common distortions include:

All-or-Nothing Thinking: Viewing yourself as either a complete success or an utter failure, with no room for middle ground.
Reality Check: Success is rarely black-and-white; growth and learning are part of the journey.

Discounting the Positive: Ignoring evidence of your achievements or brushing them off as insignificant.

Reality Check: Acknowledge and celebrate your accomplishments, no matter how small.

Catastrophizing: Expecting the worst possible outcome from any situation.

Reality Check: Most fears are exaggerated, and outcomes are often far better than anticipated.

By becoming aware of these distortions, individuals can begin to reframe their thinking and align it with reality.

3. Seeking Evidence: One effective way to counter impostor thoughts is to gather objective evidence that supports your competence. This process involves:

Documenting Achievements: Keep a record of your accomplishments, feedback, and positive outcomes as tangible proof of your skills and abilities.

Reflecting on Challenges Overcome: Consider moments when you faced adversity and succeeded. These instances highlight resilience and capability.

Seeking External Perspective: Ask trusted colleagues, mentors, or friends for their honest assessment of your contributions. Often, others see strengths you may overlook.

Evidence-based reflection helps separate impostor thoughts from the truth and builds confidence in your abilities.

4. Embracing Self-Compassion: A key step in overcoming impostor thoughts is adopting a mindset of self-compassion. This involves:

Acknowledging Imperfection: Recognize that everyone makes mistakes and has areas for growth—perfection is not a prerequisite for success.

Treating Yourself Kindly: Speak to yourself with the same encouragement and understanding you'd offer a friend facing self-doubt.

Releasing Unrealistic Standards: Let go of the need to meet impossible expectations and focus on doing your best.

Self-compassion allows individuals to accept their humanity while still striving for improvement.

5. Reframing Success and Failure: Reframe the way you view success and failure to

weaken the grip of imposter thoughts.
Consider:

Redefining Success: Success isn't about perfection or universal approval; it's about progress, impact, and personal fulfillment.

Valuing Effort over Outcome: Recognize the hard work and dedication that goes into your endeavors, regardless of the final result.

Learning from Mistakes: Rather than fearing failure, view it as an opportunity for growth and discovery.

This shift in perspective fosters resilience and confidence, even in the face of challenges.

6. Building a Supportive Mindset: Overcoming imposter syndrome requires nurturing a supportive mental environment. Steps to achieve this include:

Practicing Gratitude: Focus on the positive aspects of your life and achievements, which reinforces a sense of worthiness.

Celebrating Small Wins: Acknowledge daily successes to build momentum and confidence over time.

Avoiding Comparisons: Remember that everyone's journey is unique, and comparisons only fuel unnecessary self-doubt.

A supportive mindset creates a foundation for self-belief and empowerment.

Feeling Trapped in the Wrong Career

Feeling stuck or unfulfilled in your career is a common experience, and it can be challenging to determine whether the dissatisfaction stems from fear or a genuine mismatch with your work. Identifying the signs of career dissatisfaction and understanding the root causes is essential for making informed decisions about your professional life. Below, we'll explore how to recognize the warning signs and distinguish between fear of change and actual misalignment with your career.
Identifying Signs of Career Dissatisfaction

Career dissatisfaction doesn't always announce itself in loud, obvious ways. It often manifests subtly over time, through emotional, mental, and physical signals. Recognizing these indicators is the first step toward understanding your relationship with your job.

1. Lack of Motivation and Passion: One of the clearest signs of career dissatisfaction is a persistent lack of enthusiasm for your work. Tasks that once excited you might now feel monotonous or draining. You may find yourself:

Struggling to get out of bed or dreading the start of each workweek.

Feeling disengaged or indifferent to the outcomes of your projects.

Questioning the purpose and impact of your work.

When passion fades, it's worth considering whether your job aligns with your values and aspirations.

2. Chronic Stress and Burnout: A job that consistently leaves you feeling overwhelmed, stressed, or emotionally depleted may be a poor fit. Symptoms of burnout include:

Physical exhaustion, headaches, or sleep disturbances.

Emotional fatigue, irritability, or a sense of hopelessness.

Difficulty concentrating or staying productive.

Burnout often results from misaligned priorities, excessive demands, or a lack of balance between work and personal life.

3. Feeling Undervalued or Stagnant: Another sign of dissatisfaction is feeling unappreciated or stuck in your role. You may notice:

Limited opportunities for growth, advancement, or skill development.

Lack of recognition or acknowledgment for your contributions.

A sense that your talents and abilities are underutilized.
When a job fails to challenge or reward you, it can lead to feelings of frustration and resentment.

4. Disconnect from Values and Purpose: Your career should resonate with your personal values and sense of purpose. If it doesn't, you might experience:

A feeling that your work lacks meaning or impact.

Ethical conflicts or discomfort with the company's culture or practices.

An inner desire to pursue something more fulfilling or aligned with your passions.

A misalignment with your core values often leaves you questioning whether your current path is the right one.

5. Envy of Others' Careers: If you frequently compare your job to others' careers and feel envious or dissatisfied, it's a sign that your current role may not be meeting your needs. This doesn't mean you should measure success against others, but it's worth reflecting on what aspects of their work appeal to you.

6. Daydreaming About Quitting: While it's normal to fantasize occasionally about escaping work stress, persistent thoughts about quitting or changing careers suggest deeper dissatisfaction. If you often think, "There has to be more than this," it's time to evaluate your situation.

By acknowledging these signs, you create the opportunity to explore whether your career dissatisfaction stems from fear or genuine misalignment.
Exploring Whether It's Fear or Genuine Misalignment

Once you've recognized dissatisfaction, the next step is to determine its cause. Is it rooted in fear of change, failure, or judgment, or is it the result of a deeper disconnect between your job and your true self? Exploring these possibilities requires introspection and honesty.

1. Understanding Fear as a Barrier: Fear often disguises itself as career dissatisfaction, making it difficult to discern your true feelings. Here are some common fears that might influence your perspective:

Fear of Failure: You may feel trapped because you're afraid to take risks or fail in a new venture. This fear can make your current job feel safer, even if it's unfulfilling.

Example: Staying in a secure position despite desiring a creative or entrepreneurial path.

Fear of Judgment: Concern about how others will perceive your decisions can prevent you from pursuing changes that align with your happiness.
Example: Worrying that friends or family will view a career change as irresponsible or risky.

Fear of the Unknown: Uncertainty about what the future holds in a new job or field can make your current role feel like a comfort zone.

Example: Hesitating to leave a predictable corporate job for a freelance or unconventional career.

Fear often thrives on "what if" scenarios, creating doubts that overshadow possibilities. To confront these fears, try journaling or speaking with a trusted mentor to articulate and examine your concerns. Ask yourself:

Are my fears realistic, or are they based on assumptions or worst-case scenarios?

What's the worst that could happen if I pursued a different path, and how would I handle it?

Am I holding myself back due to fear, or are there valid reasons for staying in my current role?

2. Assessing Genuine Misalignment: True misalignment occurs when your career no longer reflects your values, interests, and

strengths. To evaluate whether this is the case, consider the following questions:

Does My Work Reflect My Passions?
If your job feels disconnected from your interests, it may signal that your career path needs adjustment.

Example: An individual passionate about environmental sustainability working in a role that lacks meaningful impact on the planet.

Am I Using My Strengths and Skills?

A role that doesn't challenge or utilize your unique abilities often leads to frustration and boredom.

Example: A creative thinker stuck in a rigid, process-driven job.

Does My Work Align with My Values?

Evaluate whether your job reflects what matters most to you, such as innovation, collaboration, or making a positive difference.

Example: Working in a high-pressure, profit-driven environment that conflicts with your desire for a balanced and ethical workplace.

Am I Growing Professionally and Personally?

A lack of growth opportunities is a strong indicator of misalignment. Ask yourself whether your role allows you to develop new skills, advance your career, or achieve your long-term goals.

Example: Feeling stagnant in a role that offers little room for upward mobility or skill enhancement.

Do I Look Forward to My Future in This Role?

If you can't envision a fulfilling future in your current career, it may be time to consider new possibilities.

Example: Realizing that your current job feels like a steppingstone rather than a destination.

3. Conducting a Reality Check: To gain clarity, balance your emotions with objective analysis. Steps include:

Reflecting on Past Decisions: Consider why you chose this career initially and whether those reasons still hold true.

Seeking Feedback: Talk to colleagues, mentors, or career coaches to gain an external perspective on your strengths and potential.

Exploring Alternatives: Research other industries or roles that align with your interests, and evaluate how they compare to your current position.

4. Testing the Waters: If you're uncertain whether dissatisfaction stems from fear or

misalignment, explore low-risk ways to test new opportunities:

Take on side projects or volunteer work that aligns with your interests.

Network with professionals in fields you're curious about to gain insight.

Pursue skill development or certifications in areas of interest to gauge your enthusiasm.

These steps allow you to explore change without fully committing, reducing the fear factor while providing valuable information about your aspirations.

Addressing Loneliness

Loneliness is a universal human experience, yet it can feel deeply personal and isolating when it occurs. It goes beyond being physically alone and often reflects a lack of meaningful connection to others or even to oneself. To address loneliness effectively, it's essential to understand its root causes and take intentional steps toward building meaningful relationships. Let's explore these two aspects in detail.
Understanding the Root Causes of Loneliness

1. Loneliness as a Multi-Faceted Experience: Loneliness is not simply about the absence of people in one's life. It is a subjective emotional state that occurs when the quality or depth of one's relationships fails to meet

their needs. This means it's possible to feel lonely even when surrounded by others if those connections lack authenticity or emotional intimacy.

2. External Root Causes of Loneliness: Several external factors contribute to loneliness, including:

Life Transitions: Significant changes, such as moving to a new city, starting a new job, or retiring, can disrupt existing social networks and create feelings of isolation.

Cultural or Social Factors: In highly individualistic societies, the focus on independence and self-reliance can reduce opportunities for meaningful community connections. Similarly, societal norms or prejudices may lead to the exclusion of marginalized groups.

Technological Influence: While technology enables instant communication, it can also foster superficial interactions that lack depth. Overreliance on social media or virtual communication can exacerbate feelings of disconnection.

Pandemics or Crises: Events such as pandemics or natural disasters often force physical distancing, limiting in-person interaction and increasing feelings of isolation.

3. Internal Root Causes of Loneliness: Beyond external circumstances, internal

factors can also play a significant role in loneliness:

Low Self-Esteem or Self-Worth: Individuals who struggle with self-esteem may believe they are unworthy of connection or feel too anxious to reach out to others.

Fear of Rejection: People who fear vulnerability or rejection may avoid seeking connections altogether, perpetuating isolation.

Unrealistic Expectations: Holding idealized standards for relationships may lead to dissatisfaction with real-life connections, fostering feelings of loneliness.

Inner Disconnect: Sometimes, loneliness stems from a disconnection with oneself. This occurs when individuals suppress their authentic emotions, values, or desires, leaving them feeling out of touch with who they are.

4. Situational Loneliness vs. Chronic Loneliness: It's important to distinguish between situational loneliness and chronic loneliness:

Situational Loneliness arises from temporary circumstances, such as a breakup, moving, or losing a loved one. While painful, this type of loneliness often resolves as circumstances improve or as new connections are formed.

Chronic Loneliness, on the other hand, persists over time and may reflect deeper underlying issues, such as emotional unavailability, prolonged isolation, or difficulty forming relationships.

Understanding the root cause of one's loneliness is the first step toward meaningful and effective solutions.
Building Meaningful Connections

Creating genuine and lasting relationships requires intentionality, vulnerability, and effort. Here are practical strategies for fostering meaningful connections:

1. Strengthening Existing Relationships: Often, deepening the connections you already have can alleviate feelings of loneliness.

Reach Out Regularly: Consistent communication strengthens bonds. A simple message or call to check in can rekindle a connection.

Share and Listen: Be open about your feelings, needs, and experiences, and actively listen when others share theirs. Emotional intimacy flourishes through mutual vulnerability.

Spend Quality Time: Prioritize meaningful activities with loved ones, such as sharing meals, going on walks, or engaging in hobbies together.

Express Gratitude: Show appreciation for the people in your life. Expressing gratitude strengthens relationships and encourages reciprocity.

2. Expanding Social Circles: If your existing connections are limited, building new relationships is essential.

Pursue Shared Interests: Join clubs, classes, or groups that align with your passions or hobbies. Shared activities provide a natural foundation for connection.

Volunteer: Helping others not only contributes to a sense of purpose but also creates opportunities to meet like-minded individuals who value community.

Attend Community Events: Local gatherings, workshops, or meetups offer opportunities to meet people in your area who share similar interests or goals.

Network Authentically: Whether professionally or personally, approach networking as an opportunity to connect rather than impress. Show genuine interest in others and cultivate relationships over time.

3. Building Deeper Connections Through Vulnerability: Depth in relationships requires vulnerability and authenticity.

Be Honest About Your Needs: Share your feelings of loneliness or desire for connection with those you trust. Often, others will reciprocate with similar experiences.

Embrace Imperfection: Authentic connections flourish when people accept each other's flaws and imperfections rather than striving for perfection.

Practice Empathy: Understanding and validating others' feelings fosters mutual trust and emotional intimacy.

4. Fostering a Sense of Belonging: Belonging comes from feeling accepted and valued within a community.

Contribute to Communities: Take active roles in social groups or organizations that matter to you. Contributing fosters a sense of purpose and integration.

Celebrate Shared Rituals: Participating in traditions, holidays, or group activities strengthens a sense of connection to others.

5. Building a Healthy Relationship with Yourself: The foundation of meaningful connections often begins with the relationship you have with yourself.

Cultivate Self-Compassion: Treat yourself with kindness and understanding, recognizing that loneliness is a shared human experience.

Develop Emotional Resilience: Learn to process emotions effectively and navigate life's challenges without relying solely on external validation.

Explore Personal Passions: Spending time doing what you love enhances your sense of fulfillment, making it easier to connect with others from a place of wholeness.

Learn to Enjoy Solitude: While loneliness is painful, solitude can be enriching. Practice mindfulness, meditation, or journaling to develop a sense of inner peace and self-awareness.

6. Seeking Professional Support: If loneliness feels overwhelming or persists despite efforts to connect, seeking professional help can provide valuable insight and tools.

Therapists or Counselors: Professionals can help identify and address internal barriers to connection, such as self-doubt, fear of rejection, or unresolved trauma.

Support Groups: Joining groups for individuals experiencing similar challenges fosters a sense of camaraderie and shared understanding.

7. Leveraging Technology Wisely: While technology can sometimes exacerbate loneliness, it can also be a powerful tool for connection when used mindfully.

Stay Connected Virtually: Use video calls, messaging apps, or social media to stay in touch with distant friends and family.

Seek Online Communities: Join forums, groups, or networks that align with your interests or values.

Limit Superficial Interaction: Focus on using technology to enhance meaningful connections rather than replacing in-person or emotional interactions.

Fear of Change

Change is an inevitable aspect of life, yet it often stirs up a whirlwind of emotions that leave many feeling resistant or even paralyzed. The fear of change arises from our natural aversion to uncertainty and discomfort, making it one of the most common psychological hurdles. However, with the right perspective, change can be reframed as a gateway to growth and opportunity. Let's explore why change feels daunting, how resistance manifests, and how to approach change in a constructive way. Why Change Is Daunting and How Resistance Manifests

1. Innate Preference for Familiarity Human beings are hardwired to seek safety in predictability. Evolutionarily speaking, routines and familiarity were crucial for survival, allowing early humans to navigate their environment with minimal risk. Change

disrupts this sense of stability, triggering our brain's alarm system—the amygdala—which perceives uncertainty as a potential threat. While this response was beneficial in the past, it often overreacts in modern contexts where change is rarely life-threatening.

At its core, the fear of change is rooted in the unknown. When faced with new situations, people often ask themselves:

What if I fail?

What if I make the wrong choice?

What if things get worse instead of better?

These questions reflect our natural inclination to anticipate worst-case scenarios, amplifying the emotional weight of change.

2. Loss Aversion Another reason change is daunting is the psychological principle of loss aversion. People tend to fear losing what they already have more than they value the potential to gain something new. For instance:

Leaving a stable job for a new, untested opportunity can feel risky, even if the new role offers better growth potential.

Moving to a different city may evoke fears of losing close friendships and community ties.

This tendency to focus on potential losses often blinds individuals to the opportunities that change might bring.

3. Emotional Attachment to the Status Quo The familiarity of the status quo creates a sense of comfort, even if the current situation is less than ideal. For example:

Staying in an unfulfilling relationship may feel safer than confronting the uncertainty of being single.

Remaining in a stagnant career may feel easier than the effort required to explore new paths.

This emotional attachment reinforces a preference for sticking with what is known, even at the cost of personal growth.

4. Fear of Failure and Judgment Change often requires taking risks, and with risk comes the possibility of failure. Fear of failure can be overwhelming, as it challenges one's self-esteem and sense of competence. Additionally, the fear of judgment from others can further deter individuals from embracing change. People may worry about being criticized for their choices, which creates additional pressure to maintain the status quo.

5. Resistance Through Procrastination and Avoidance Resistance to change often manifests in subtle yet powerful ways, such as procrastination or avoidance. Instead of

actively confronting the need for change, individuals may:

Delay making decisions, hoping circumstances will resolve themselves.

Distract themselves with other tasks to avoid dealing with uncertainty.

Rationalize inaction with excuses like "The timing isn't right" or "It's too risky right now."

This resistance creates a cycle of stagnation, where fear-driven inaction prevents growth and reinforces feelings of being stuck.

6. Psychological and Emotional Effects of Resistance The resistance to change can take a toll on emotional and mental well-being. It often leads to:

Chronic stress and anxiety, as unresolved decisions weigh heavily on the mind.

Frustration and self-doubt, stemming from a lack of progress or perceived inability to overcome fear.

Resentment toward oneself or others for missed opportunities or unfulfilled potential.

Recognizing these manifestations of resistance is the first step toward understanding and addressing the fear of change.
Reframing Change as an Opportunity

While the fear of change is natural, it doesn't have to be debilitating. By shifting perspectives and adopting constructive approaches, individuals can view change as a catalyst for growth and possibility rather than a source of fear.

1. Redefining Change One of the most effective ways to reframe change is to redefine what it means. Instead of perceiving change as a disruption, think of it as:

A Chance for Growth: Change provides opportunities to learn, develop new skills, and expand your horizons.

Example: Starting a new job may feel intimidating, but it can also introduce you to exciting challenges and professional growth.

A Fresh Start: Change allows you to let go of old patterns, relationships, or situations that no longer serve you, paving the way for a more fulfilling life.

An Exploration of Potential: Embracing change opens doors to possibilities that you might never have considered before.

By focusing on the positive aspects of change, you can reduce the emotional weight of fear and approach it with curiosity and optimism.

2. Breaking Change into Manageable Steps The enormity of change can feel

overwhelming, but breaking it into smaller, manageable steps makes it more approachable. For example:

Instead of "Change my career," start with researching potential fields or attending a networking event.

Instead of "Transform my health," begin with incorporating one new habit, such as drinking more water or walking for 10 minutes a day.

Taking incremental actions builds momentum and confidence, making the process of change feel less daunting.

3. Challenging Limiting Beliefs Fear of change is often fueled by limiting beliefs, such as:

"I'm not capable of handling this."

"It's too late to start over."

"What if I regret my decision?"

Challenge these beliefs by asking yourself:

"What evidence supports this fear, and what evidence contradicts it?"

"What's the worst that could happen, and how would I cope with it?"

"What's the best that could happen, and how would that improve my life?"

Reframing limiting beliefs empowers you to approach change with a growth mindset rather than a fear-based one.

4. Cultivating a Growth Mindset A growth mindset is the belief that abilities, skills, and intelligence can be developed through effort and learning. This mindset encourages viewing change as:

An Opportunity to Adapt: Challenges are seen as chances to grow stronger and more resilient.

A Path to Mastery: Even failures are valuable experiences that contribute to long-term success.

Adopting a growth mindset helps you focus on progress rather than perfection, making change feel like a rewarding journey rather than a daunting task.

5. Seeking Support and Building Resilience Facing change doesn't mean going it alone. Building a support network of friends, family, mentors, or therapists can provide encouragement and guidance. Additionally, resilience can be strengthened through practices such as:

Mindfulness and Stress Management: Techniques like meditation or deep breathing help calm the mind and reduce fear-driven responses.

Gratitude: Focusing on what you're grateful for fosters a positive outlook, even during uncertain times.

Reflection and Self-Compassion: Journaling or self-reflecting allows you to acknowledge progress and accept setbacks without judgment.

6. Focusing on Long-Term Benefits When fear of change arises, it's helpful to visualize the long-term benefits of embracing it. Ask yourself:

"How will this change improve my life a year from now?"

"What opportunities will I miss if I don't take this step?"

Keeping your focus on the potential rewards can motivate you to move forward, even when the journey feels uncertain.

CHAPTER 3

Silencing Fear

Shifting Mindsets

Changing the way you think is a crucial part of silencing fear and regaining control of your life. A significant part of this involves cultivating self-compassion and self-acceptance, as well as learning to replace limiting beliefs with empowering ones. These shifts in mindset not only dismantle fear-based thinking but also pave the way for personal growth and resilience.
The Importance of Self-Compassion and Self-Acceptance

1. What Is Self-Compassion and Why Does It Matter? Self-compassion is the act of treating yourself with the same kindness, care, and understanding you would offer to a dear friend. It involves acknowledging your struggles without harsh self-criticism and embracing your humanity, imperfections and all. In the face of fear, self-compassion acts as a buffer, helping you navigate challenges with a sense of calm and self-support.

Self-compassion matters because:

It Reduces Fear and Anxiety: When you treat yourself kindly, you shift your focus from self-judgment to self-care, reducing the mental strain that fear imposes.

It Builds Resilience: Self-compassion strengthens your ability to recover from setbacks, making you better equipped to handle life's uncertainties.

It Promotes Emotional Well-Being: A compassionate mindset fosters feelings of contentment, gratitude, and self-worth, which can counteract fear-based emotions like inadequacy and self-doubt.

2. The Role of Self-Acceptance in Silencing Fear Self-acceptance is the practice of embracing yourself fully, including your strengths, weaknesses, and flaws. Fear often thrives on self-criticism and the unrealistic expectation that you need to be perfect to succeed. By accepting yourself as you are, you silence the inner critic that amplifies your fears.

Key benefits of self-acceptance include:

Freedom from Perfectionism: Self-acceptance allows you to take risks without the pressure of being flawless, reducing fear of failure.

Authenticity and Confidence: When you accept yourself, you feel more comfortable being genuine, which builds confidence and reduces fear of judgment.

Inner Peace: Accepting your past mistakes and limitations helps you let go of shame and guilt, creating a sense of peace and emotional stability.

3. Practicing Self-Compassion and Self-Acceptance

Acknowledge Your Feelings: When fear arises, instead of suppressing it, recognize it as a natural human emotion. Say to yourself, "It's okay to feel this way right now."

Be Kind to Yourself: Replace harsh self-criticism with supportive statements. For instance, instead of thinking, "I'll never be good enough," tell yourself, "I'm doing the best I can, and that's enough."

Reflect on Shared Humanity: Remind yourself that fear and imperfection are universal. Everyone experiences setbacks and struggles—it's part of being human.

Celebrate Your Strengths: Regularly reflect on your achievements and qualities that make you unique, focusing on what you appreciate about yourself.

By embracing self-compassion and self-acceptance, you create a foundation of emotional safety and self-worth, making it easier to confront and overcome fear. Replacing Limiting Beliefs with Empowering Ones

1. Understanding Limiting Beliefs and Their Effects Limiting beliefs are deeply ingrained thoughts or assumptions that constrain your potential and keep you tethered to fear. These beliefs often stem from past

experiences, societal conditioning, or self-doubt. Examples of limiting beliefs include:

"I'm not talented enough to succeed."

"If I fail, everyone will think I'm a fraud."

"I'm too old to start something new."

The effects of limiting beliefs can be profound:

Self-Sabotage: Limiting beliefs create a mental barrier that prevents you from pursuing opportunities or taking risks.

Insecurity and Fear: These beliefs reinforce feelings of inadequacy and amplify fears of failure, rejection, or judgment.

Stagnation: By convincing yourself that change isn't possible, you remain stuck in unfulfilling situations.

Recognizing and challenging these beliefs is essential for breaking free from fear.

2. The Power of Empowering Beliefs
Empowering beliefs are thoughts that inspire confidence, hope, and action. They replace fear-driven assumptions with positive, growth-oriented perspectives. Examples of empowering beliefs include:

"I am capable of learning and growing from any challenge."

"Failure is just a steppingstone to success."

"I have the strength to overcome obstacles and create the life I want."

By cultivating empowering beliefs, you reframe fear as an opportunity rather than a threat, enabling you to approach life with optimism and courage.

3. Steps to Replace Limiting Beliefs

Identify Your Limiting Beliefs: Begin by reflecting on the fears that hold you back. Ask yourself:

What thoughts arise when I face challenges or uncertainty?

Do these thoughts encourage or discourage me?

Are they based on facts or assumptions?

Example: If you think, "I'll never be good at public speaking," identify it as a limiting belief tied to fear of failure or judgment.

Challenge the Validity of These Beliefs: Once you've identified a limiting belief, examine whether it's truly valid. Ask yourself:

What evidence supports this belief?

What evidence contradicts it?

Is this belief based on a past experience that no longer applies?

Example: You may realize that your fear of public speaking is based on one awkward presentation years ago, despite receiving positive feedback in more recent situations.

Reframe Limiting Beliefs into Empowering Ones: Transform negative assumptions into positive affirmations that encourage action. For instance:

Limiting belief: "I'll never be good at public speaking."

Empowering belief: "With practice and preparation, I can become a confident and effective speaker."

By reframing your perspective, you create a mental shift that reduces fear and builds confidence.

Take Small, Meaningful Actions: Empowering beliefs are reinforced through action. Start by taking small steps that challenge your fears and prove your capabilities. For example:

If you fear public speaking, begin by speaking in front of a small, supportive group before gradually increasing your audience size.

Each action strengthens your belief in your ability to overcome challenges.

Surround Yourself with Positivity: Surrounding yourself with supportive and encouraging individuals can help reinforce empowering beliefs. Seek out mentors, friends, or communities that uplift and inspire you to grow.

Practice Affirmations and Visualization: Daily affirmations and visualization exercises can help solidify empowering beliefs. For instance, repeat statements like:

"I am capable of achieving my goals."

"I embrace challenges as opportunities for growth."

Visualize yourself succeeding in situations that currently trigger fear, creating a mental blueprint for success.

4. Overcoming Resistance to Change
Replacing limiting beliefs requires patience and persistence. It's normal to feel resistance or doubt during the process. Combat this resistance by:

Celebrating Progress: Acknowledge each step forward, no matter how small. Progress is a testament to your strength and resilience.

Practicing Self-Compassion: Be kind to yourself when setbacks occur. Remind yourself that growth is a journey, not a destination.

Staying Committed: Replacing limiting beliefs is a gradual process. Consistent effort and reflection will yield lasting change.

CHAPTER 4

Winning the Mental Game

Self-Discovery

Self-discovery is a cornerstone of taking control of your life and silencing fear. It involves peeling back the layers of societal expectations, fears, and external influences to identify your core values, passions, and purpose. This awareness gives you a clearer direction, enabling you to make decisions aligned with your authentic self. Let's explore how to identify personal values and passions, along with practical exercises to help clarify your purpose.

Identifying Personal Values and Passions

1. What Are Personal Values? Personal values are the principles and beliefs that guide your actions, decisions, and priorities. They reflect what truly matters to you and serve as a compass for your behavior. Examples of values include:

Integrity

Freedom

Creativity

Family

Growth

Adventure

When your life aligns with your values, you're more likely to feel fulfilled and at peace. Conversely, a disconnect between your actions and values often leads to dissatisfaction and inner conflict.

2. How to Identify Your Values Identifying your values requires introspection and honesty. Here's how:

Reflect on Peak Moments: Think about times when you felt truly happy, proud, or fulfilled. What values were being honored in those moments? For example, if you felt proud after mentoring someone, you might value contribution or leadership.

Consider What Angers You: Reflect on situations that frustrate or upset you. These often point to violated values. For instance, if dishonesty angers you, integrity may be a core value.

Prioritize Values: Create a list of potential values (e.g., freedom, security, connection) and rank them in order of importance. This exercise clarifies what drives you most.

3. Understanding Passions Passions are activities, interests, or topics that energize and inspire you. They are often things you lose track of time doing or subjects you could explore endlessly. Passions bring joy and meaning to life and can guide you toward fulfilling pursuits.

4. How to Identify Your Passions To uncover your passions:

Recall Childhood Interests: What activities brought you joy as a child? Often, childhood passions reflect unfiltered interests before societal expectations intervened.

Notice What Excites You: Pay attention to tasks, topics, or conversations that ignite your enthusiasm or curiosity.

Evaluate What You're Willing to Struggle For: Passions are not always effortless. Ask yourself, "What challenges am I willing to embrace because the reward is worth it?" For example, an aspiring author might endure the frustrations of writer's block because they're passionate about storytelling.

Exercises for Clarifying Your Purpose

Once you've identified your values and passions, the next step is to clarify how these elements come together to define your purpose. Purpose provides a sense of direction and motivation, helping you navigate life's challenges with intention.

1. The Values and Passions Alignment Exercise This exercise helps you connect your values and passions to potential purpose-driven goals:

List Your Top Five Values: Use the steps above to identify the values that resonate most with you.

List Your Top Five Passions: Identify the activities or interests that bring you joy and energy.

Find Overlap: Look for intersections between your values and passions. For example:

Value: Contribution

Passion: Writing

Overlap: Writing books or articles that inspire positive change.

Brainstorm Applications: Explore ways to align your passions and values with actionable goals or careers. Ask yourself:

How can I use my passions to honor my values?

What roles or activities align with this intersection?

2. The Five Whys Exercise This exercise helps you dig deeper into your motivations and uncover your purpose:

Start with a goal or activity you're drawn to. For example, "I want to start a business."

Ask why this goal matters to you and write down your answer.

For each answer, ask why again. Repeat this process five times.

By the fifth "why," you'll often uncover a deeper, more meaningful reason behind your goal.

Example:

I want to start a business. (Why?)

To have more freedom over my time. (Why?)

So I can spend more time with my family. (Why?)

Because I want to create lasting memories with them. (Why?)

Because family is my top priority. In this example, the purpose is not just about starting a business—it's about prioritizing family and creating a life of balance and connection.

3. The Ikigai Exercise (Finding Your "Reason for Being") This Japanese concept combines four elements to clarify your purpose:

What You Love: List activities or topics you're passionate about.

What You're Good At: Identify your skills and strengths.

What the World Needs: Reflect on issues or needs you care about solving.

What You Can Be Paid For: Consider ways to monetize your passions or skills.

Diagram the Overlap: Create a diagram with four circles representing these elements. Where the circles overlap is your "ikigai," or purpose.

Example Application:

What you love: Teaching and storytelling.

What you're good at: Communication and empathy.

What the world needs: Accessible education for underserved communities.

What you can be paid for: Online courses or mentorship programs. Purpose: Becoming an educator or mentor to empower underserved communities.

4. Visualization for Purpose Clarity Visualization involves imagining your ideal life and using this mental image to guide your purpose:

Close Your Eyes and Visualize: Picture yourself 5–10 years in the future, living a fulfilled and meaningful life. Consider:

What are you doing?

Who are you surrounded by?

What impact are you making?

Write Down the Details: Capture your vision in writing to solidify your clarity.

Identify Themes: Look for recurring themes or values in your vision. For instance:

If your vision involves helping others, contribution may be a core value.

If it includes creative projects, creativity may drive your purpose.

5. Legacy Reflection Exercise Reflecting on the legacy you want to leave can also clarify your purpose:

Imagine Your Eulogy: What would you want people to say about you at the end of your life? Consider:

How did you impact others?

What did you contribute to the world?

What values defined your life?

Write Your Desired Legacy: Use this reflection to identify the values, passions, and goals that align with the legacy you wish to create.

Bringing Self-Discovery to Life

Self-discovery is an ongoing journey, and each exercise deepens your understanding of your values, passions, and purpose. Here are additional tips to integrate your discoveries into daily life:

Create an Action Plan: Use your insights to set specific, achievable goals that align with your values and passions.

Stay Open to Growth: Your purpose may evolve over time. Continue exploring new interests and adjusting your path as needed.

Celebrate Progress: Acknowledge each step you take toward living authentically, no matter how small.

Seek Support: Surround yourself with people who encourage your journey and share your aspirations.

THE END

Printed in Great Britain
by Amazon

61441643R00038